THE BLUE BOOK

To my parents

owen sheers

THE BLUE BOOK

seren

Seren is the book imprint of
Poetry Wales Press Ltd.
57 Nolton Street, Bridgend, Wales, CF31 3AE
01656 663018
www.seren-books.com

© Owen Sheers, 2000
Reprinted 2000 (twice), 2002, 2004, 2008
www.owen-sheers.com

ISBN 1-85411-277-5

A CIP record for this title is available from the British Library

The publisher acknowledges the financial assistance
of the Welsh Books Council

Owen Sheers' eye photographed by Anna Saltmarsh

Printed in Palatino by CPD Limited, Blaenau Gwent

Contents

Feeling the Catch

It is four in the morning, and one lamp strobes me in its
                                                   stutter,
the only sound, its filament fizzing, popping, fizzing
as last night's rain slugs by in the gutter.

I am by the pub where things happened first:
the hot flush of whisky down the back of my neck,
the quick release in the alley out back.

There is a body shifting on the step of the doorway,
deep in its sleeping bag, a draft excluder caught the
                                                   wrong side;
a dirty blue chrysalis of dreams and cold.

But all I can think of is the heat in there,
the press of dancing bodies, the sheen of sweat,
piss steaming in a full ceramic sink,

three men round it, looking down, hands in front,
like picketing workers round a brazier
or bowed head mourners at a funeral sermon.

And of Dai, doing his flaming Drambuies,
head back, eyes to the ceiling, mouth open wide,
singing hot notes of blue flickering flame.

How he used to make us lower the match
that lit the pink, ribbed roof of his mouth,
before it caught and he felt the catch;

a flame from nowhere,
hot on his lips, which he would shut with a snap,
careful not to burn himself on his own blue breath.

And then his gasp, his long outward sigh,
and the shake of his head, like a horse,
bluebottles caught in its eye.

*

And now here, on this hill, where I came with you,
the girl in the red dress whose name I can't remember,
on the only night we ever spoke.

Lying back on the bonnet of your father's car,
watching the house lights strike off,
shrinking the town to its tight centre.

Then looking up, constellations growing on the night sky;
following the curves of slow satellites
or the quicker release of meteorites: eighteen that night.

I never did see that dress, or you again.
Some told me it was because you were with Dai,
although I never knew and you never said,

but I still like to think I made an impression,
or at least left a reminder in the shallow dent
in the finish of your father's car —

right where it's hardest to beat out.

*

This was where Dai came too, eighteen that day,
stopping above the valley's river of lights.

Unscrewing the cap like a bottle of squash,
and pouring it out over his thighs,

lifting it, so it ran, thick over his head,
hair slicked down, an otter rising through water.

Then he must have lowered the match, careful,
waiting for the quick release and the catch,

8

which when it came set his body alive with fire,
flames quick at his finger tips, hot on his lips,

peeling at his skin, turning his hair to magnesium strips,
which fizz, then pop, then fizz.

The car windows shatter,
shooting stars out,

glass constellations growing on the dark tarmac
with each pane's crack and burst,

while Dai, head back, mouth open wide,
burns himself on his own blue breath.

Coming Home

My mother's hug is awkward,
as if the space between her open arms
is reserved for a child, not this body of a man.
In the kitchen she kneads the dough,
flipping it and patting before laying in again.
The flour makes her over, dusting
the hairs on her cheek, smoothing out wrinkles.

*

Dad still goes and soaks himself in the rain.
Up to his elbows in hedge, he works
on a hole that reappears every Winter,
its edges laced with wet wool —
frozen breaths snagged on the blackthorn.
When he comes in again his hair is wild,
and his pockets are filled with filings of hay.

*

All seated, my grandfather pours the wine.
His unsteady hand makes the neck of the bottle
shiver on the lip of each glass;
it is a tune he plays faster each year.

Hedge Foal

At first we saw just the mare,
her swollen stomach deflated,
the wax on her teats broken,
standing, head low, by the hedge,
waiting for something to happen.

Then the afterbirth, discarded by her side:
a jelly fish placenta,
its bloody tentacles and loose, clear skin
slick over dock leaves and nettles.
The bitten umbilical cord like red steel rope.

And then finally, the foal,
cast deep in the hedge,
where it had rolled down the slope,
finding its all-hinge legs too collapsible
and its pulpy hooves too soft.

Suspended in blackthorn,
hung by bindatwine round its lips,
pulling them forward to a pucker.
Still and patient; an embryo
awaiting its birth back into the field.

Training in Blaina

When the floods were down
we parked the cars on four sides,
and trained in the cross-fire of headlights,
their beams cutting compass points.

Once I arrived early,
to find Gareth doing sprints in the river,
pushing himself in slow motion
through the waist-high water.

Taking on the current with busy arms,
before easing, and letting it nudge him
back to his starting place, where he turns,
chasing the water upstream once more.

Old Horse, New Tricks

The vet was careful
to place the barrel of his gun
right on the swirl of hair
in the centre of her forehead.

In the silence after the explosion
she was still for a second,
as if she would stand in death
as she had stood in sleep.

We watched, an audience expecting tricks,
and eventually she obliged,
succumbing to the slow fold of her fall
with a buckling of the crooked back legs

and a comedy sideways lean that went too far.
There was little symmetry in her collapse,
just the natural pattern of pain.
Even her tongue was out of order,

escaping from the side of her jaw,
and dipping to taste the earth below,
like a child, stealing a taste of the cake
before it is served.

Stammerer on Scree

This slope is my language.
A shifting skin of stone
that slips under my grip,
feet pedalling the one moving spot,
sharded slate, flowing hard water.

But when I am still,
crabbed against its steepness,
cheek to its side, a child on its mother,
then it stops.
Stone-ticks out to quiet,
rests itself on the mountain,
meaning everything.

Until I move again,
when it spreads under my hand,
slides from under my climbing feet,
like words from under a memory,
vowels from under a tongue.

Unfinished Business

We often saw him pass the classroom window,

bunking off, jumper alive with ferrets,
two thin dogs snapping round the hem of his coat.

At fifteen he bolted from a tattoo parlour,
down on the docks in Swansea;

bursting into the light before the tattooist could start the S,
sprinting down the street, ATAN still bleeding on his head.

He tried to make sense of it in biro,
appearing at the gates, the crucial letter scratched in,

and despite our fear (we knew he'd dropped
a breeze block onto some bloke's unconscious face,

attacked a teacher with a Stanley knife, threatened
to fill in his kids and fuck his wife) we still laughed;

though it was always he who provided the punch lines —
usually ten or twenty times before someone could drag
                                                    him off.

Lambing

My father gloves himself in her,
up to his elbow, on his knees,
head angled, cheek resting
on the sprung wool of her rump.
Looking for coins down the back of a sofa.

His invisible fingers work inside,
finding a tangle of swollen joints
and crooked legs.
The hooves, soft as plums.

And then the slow, hydraulic extraction,
Chinese eyes and long ears pulled back
by the g-force of the womb.
The tight cling-film of the amniotic sac,

the pre-packaging of birth,
which, when it comes,
falls, flat and bloody as road kill —
a glued body, trailing a placenta,

a still life, until, at last, the first breath,
which arrives from nowhere —
an electric shock
run across the railings of its ribs.

Harvest

for S.

Sitting beneath the horse chestnut tree
we were surprised by a fall of conkers.
Miniature mines, through fathoms of leaves,
pelting our backs and our shoulders.
You began to gather them in,
squeezing out their secrets,
and those you picked you kept,
holding them tight to your stomach,
as if you had been stabbed, and were
bleeding conkers from the wound.
When they became too many,
you trusted me with some, which I held,
a bunch of knuckles in my fist.
But my sweat dulled their sheen,
turned them, dark liver brown to faded bay,
and when I gave them back to you,
you said it would always be this way;
because I am a man, and I have acid hands.

Cultivation

"I saw him run after a gilded butterfly; and when he caught it...
he did so tear it with his teeth."
— Coriolanus, I iii

When he was young, he cultivated butterflies.
Watched the slow hatching
of the paper lampshade larvae,
giving birth to hanging candelabras
of dusty, patterned satin.

He would let them fill their wings,
with fluid, with light,
and then some day, as they blinked
in the sun, he would take one
and tear it with his teeth.

Now he is grown, and I still watch him,
in the lamplight of the street.
An expert in his field, he works,
an arm about her shoulder,
a fingertip touching her cheek.

But he knows some day he will take her too,
and cultivate her skin
into a pattern of dusty bruises,
black on red, like the marks
of an Admiral's wing.

News of the World

"She was the kind of girl who made the *News of the World*,
you could say she was attractively built."
— The Beatles, "Polythene Pam"

She was the chip-shop owner's daughter,
working on Saturdays,
skin under a thin veil of sweat,
one dark curl, twisting from under her cap.

When she left we missed her mascared lashes,
her chequered dress, the flash of breast
as she dipped to shovel chips,
shaking off the scoop and wrapping them,
hot and heavy in our hands.

The next we heard was in the *News of the World*,
one grainy photo of curls and long legs;
ASCOT RACES "LADY" REVEALS ALL!

She came back once, quiet at the wheel
of her convertible, dark hair all over her face.
Friends showed her the clippings they'd kept,
when they met for a drink. Sat round her,
asking for her views on the world.

The Blue Book

"**Blue Books, The** (3 vols., 1847). Reports published by the Government on the state of education in Wales... the Commissioners reported that the common people were dirty, lazy, ignorant, superstitious, deceitful, promiscuous and immoral, and they blamed all this on Nonconformity and the Welsh language." — *Encyclopedia of Welsh Literature*

Lingen, Symons and Johnson,
their names give them away,
holding thumb-cornered text books,
not a word of Welsh between them.
Page or man.

They found their God spoken in words
that ran unnaturally in their ears,
and they wrote their decree.
Rather silence than these corrupt tongues,
the words of the father shall not be passed on to the sons.

*

Because this is how an empire is claimed
not just with stakes in stolen land,
but with words grown over palates,
with strength of tongue as well as strength of hand.

*

And now another blue book
this, my brother's school book
(bill-postered with bands, but blue beneath)
and inside, the Welsh in his and his teacher's hand.

It has fallen open on a half-written page,
the space beneath his work shot across with red pen:
"Pam nad yw hyn wedi ei orffen?"
"Why is this not finished?"

Well, maybe it is now, if not in me, then in him,
my brother, ten years younger,
but a hundred and fifty years and one tongue apart.

Learning the Language

Beneath the old oak in Llanddewi,
its tiny brains of mistletoe
showing in silhouette against the white sky;

this was where to find them.
Hard knots of hair and mucus
the paper twistings of a nervous hand,

packaged and pulled in the guts of an owl,
dropped with an upward swallow,
a single feathered heartbeat in the throat.

They translate in the warm water,
unfurl and loosen their fibres,
disclosing broken histories of bone;

a few lines of vertebrae, the clipping of a claw,
the greased and shrunken feather of a finch,
the miniature hinge of a shrew's jaw.

Laying out their patterns beneath the bright lamp,
I try to piece it together on the damp black paper —
arranging death sentences.

The Pond

This place where I took things,
sunk shallow in the middle of the field,
a secret bruise hidden by trees.

Where I brought my grandfather's death,
sucking squash from a shrinking carton,
while the tears dryed to slug lines over my cheeks.

And my first kiss, in the arched iron cow-shed,
gum-stitched and tense,
as the light faded and the farms lit up.

Where I carried my arguments,
vowing never to return, hunching under the oak,
only to slink back

through the long grass, brushing up to my knees,
when the cold had dug deep in my bones
and my anger had evolved into hunger.

Not Yet My Mother

Yesterday I found a photo
of you at seventeen,
holding a horse and smiling,
not yet my mother.

The tight riding hat hid your hair,
and your legs were still the long shins of a boy's.
You held the horse by the halter,
your hand a fist under its huge jaw.

The blown trees were still in the background
and the sky was grained by the old film stock,
but what caught me was your face,
which was mine.

And I thought, just for a second, that you were me.
But then I saw the woman's jacket,
nipped at the waist, the ballooned jodhpurs,
and of course the date, scratched in the corner.

All of which told me again,
that this was you at seventeen, holding a horse
and smiling, not yet my mother,
although I was clearly already your child.

Iron Filings

Tad Cu showed me how they bristled
under the attraction of the magnet.
From flat horse hair to close-cropped mane
in one easy slide of the hand.

When he was ill, and staying with us
he left them lying in the sink,
dark decorations against the white enamel,
stuck in the whipped cream drops of shaving foam
and clustered on the magnetic blade of his razor.

At his funeral the congregation rose to sing,
thin-leaved hymn books shaking in their hands,
before all going flat again,
under the fall of an iron Amen.

My Grandfather's Garden

Where bloodshot apples peered from the grass
and seed packets taught me the patience
of waiting through a season.

Where I cracked the seams of pods,
and fired out peas with a thumbnail
pushed along the down of the soft inside.

Where he kept order with hoe prods
at the stems of lettuces, emerging like
overgrown moth-eaten flowers, colours drained.

Where I crouched on the shed's corrugate roof,
touching ripe damsons, which fell into the lap
of my stretched T-shirt.

Where I have come now, a month after his death,
the house and garden following him out of my life,
to cut back brambles and pack away tools.

Where, entering the hollow socket of the shed,
I hear damsons tap the roof,
telling me there is no one to catch them.

War Wound

It looks old, this scar,
this trickle of raised flesh
running the length of her shin.

Yet I know it still opens daily,
seeps into her talk,
bleeding memories

of the shard that entered her leg,
and stuck out,
a gun metal fin:

of the oiled sea made slow,
with waves that heaved
and swallowed men whole:

of the officers undoing their ties
before jumping, leaving
the bed-ridden patients,

some quiet, some screaming.
And of how she saw it;
a scar across the ocean,

a disturbance on the radar,
an explosion flipping out shock waves
that never stopped.

When You Died

I ran to the top of a hill
and sat on its broken skull
of stone and wind-thinned soil.
I watched the Black Mountains darken
and the river slip the grip of the town.

I went to the pond,
the one in the field above the house,
its borders churned to mud by the cattle.
I thought of how we skated there,
taking the risk, despite the sound of the ice,
creaking like a boat's wet rigging.

I went to your house,
and saw the long, low chicken sheds.
I remembered your voice behind me,
as I, afraid of the sudden peck,
stretched my hand into the dark
to take the warm eggs, one of them
wearing a feather.

Like Sowing Seed

I

I was always surprised by their number,
tripping from the low sheds.
Their lives of short panic shocked me.

Nervous eyes, stuttering heads,
the dangerous spurs of the cockerel;
his double chin of raw skin,
rippling when he walked.

Grab a fist full, then bend the wrist out quick,
fanning the fingers wide.
Like sowing seed.

Except these grains grew instantly,
sprang into a livewire line of chickens,
nit-picking with their beaks,
stabbing the ground.

Drilling their hunger into the soil.

II

The box of ashes was too small to be you,
so I would not believe the plaque on the lid,
but still picked my fist of soil and threw.

I sometimes wish that we had fought...

I sometimes wish that we had fought
and turned our backs before you died.

That some tinder-dry idea had caught,
and flung into a rage between us,

a chest-bred passion so fierce
you lived to the extent of your living,

firing me with your eyes, banishing me
with the full depth of your voice.

That we had put distance between us,
and had not been reduced to the drawing apart

of two hands across a table.
That I had kept myself away,

where I would be deaf to the fading of your song,
where I would know that you had been;

but not that you are gone.

His and Hers

Her Memories of Him

An old man's frown on a young boy's skin.
His comfort with her caress.
A flat back and a flat chest,
wrists that went the length of his arms.

Then holding him afterwards,
feeling him shrink from her,
ebbing away inside her half open fist,
like sand disappearing through fingers.

His Memories of Her

The dryer-singed hair of his mother.
The petal-crushed smell of his sister.
The touch that was both teacher and lover.

And then, as the plane tilted away,
her hand from the next seat, pressing his thigh,
as she might a fruit, checking for ripeness.

Patchworks

She has always translated life like this;
taking the fragments, the scraps
and sealing their frayed edges

under the stutter of her old Singer.
Building houses and streets in a way
that made sense to her,

then was clear to others, who stepping back
allowed the scene to focus
out of the piecemeal canvas.

So it is no surprise to find her now,
surrounded by past works,
examining them with a halogen lamp

and the bulbous vision of a magnifier.
She is arranging them,
finding their meaning once more,

before the scraps of cataract on her cornea
join across the clear of her pupil
as they have already in the other eye —

blank behind a slow patch,
sewn there with stitches of wrinkles.

Antonia's Story

She told me how she fell to sleep with the sound of his fists
on the door.
Dull thuds that echoed on the stairs,
that became the beat of her heart on the sheet,
the rustle of blood in her ear on the pillow, then sleep.

Of how she slept a dark sleep with only one dream,
of an apple ripening, then falling a fall.
Its loud thud echoing on in the night
in the beat of her heart on the sheet.

And how she woke to the sound of fists on the door
and how she was surprised by the persistence of love.

She told me how she answered the door, and how she
saw him over the policeman's shoulder, lying on the lawn,
and how she thought why is he lying on the lawn, so pale
and quiet?
Why is he lying asleep and covered in dew?

And then how she saw the broken drainpipe he had tried
to climb,
and how she knew he had fallen, ripe in the night,
from the broken drainpipe, which still swung wild,
a madman's finger preaching in the wind.

And then she told me how now each night she unlocks
the door,
which sometimes gets blown, wild in the wind.
How her feet echo, dull on the stairs, as she climbs to bed
where she falls to sleep, the rustle of blood in her ear.

And how each night she sleeps a dark sleep with only
one dream,
of an apple, which falls, ripe in the night.
And of how she wakes with the beat of her heart on the sheet,
surprised by the persistence of love.

Twisted

When the bulb of swelling ebbed
it left the click and tut of a piece out of line;
a tag of gristle, nicked by the ankle's
ball joint roll.

It is a sound that follows me,
down long corridors,
over morning beaches
through the dark of strangers' houses.

It is the switch I flick under my skin
with every step forwards.
The searching tick of a blind man's stick,
a counting machine at the heel.

It is the sound, at dawn, of straw
caught in the plague wagon's wheel.

Harris

If it snows enough, and the wind is strong,
you can walk along the top of a hedge,
and think you're on the ground,
as Harris did, who'd lived here all his life.

It was in those lanes he was found last year,
the drifts shouldering the hedges,
echoing along the curve of the field,
lying on his back, a duvet of snow across his chest.

He was the last Council worker to mow by hand,
embroidering the banks,
skirting the primroses with his blade,
leaving the foxgloves standing tall, purple lips wide.

Now, he smiled at the sky, his eyebrows growing
thicker and whiter in the evening frost.
The crows had kissed him blind,
decorating his shroud of shifting snow
with two dark poppies, congealed on his cheek.

Harris in the Park

The girls are newly peeled.
He can sense the careless flick of their hair,
smell the lotion, rubbed deep in their skin,

across the blush of their shoulders,
while on the banks of the river
he hears the turning of pages,

or is it the leaves,
shuffling themselves through
the branches of the trees?

A bird tunes itself in,
and punters stroke their poles
through water.

The click of cricket is answered by
the metronome tick, tick, tick
of his white cane on the path.

To the Other Side with Harris

You have lent me your hand
to cross the road.
That is kind, but it is
not what I want.

Your skin is soft,
fingers like silk
against the bark
of my calluses.

You don't understand (do you?)
what you hold is my eye.
I want you to lead me
further than the other side.

I want to see the slopes
of your shoulders
lead into the delicate neck.

I want to follow the line of your back
watch long muscles
flex in your thigh.

I want to see the press of your breasts
against your dress, which must be
moulded to you by this breeze,

showing the disappearing of your waist
before the widening of your hips.
Two beautiful brackets holding their secret.

We reach the other side
and you leave me.

My French Great Aunt

I was seven when I first saw her,
a basket of cherries filling her embrace,
red gloss and green stalks piled high,
some paired; marbles of blood wishboned together.

She was my grandmother's twin,
right down to the wrinkles etched over her eyes
so I was surprised by the sound of French in her mouth,
her stranger's look, the lightness of her hand on my head.

Years later, on our way to visit friends in Nice,
we stopped at a house in the country,
where tall trees cast shadows over shaven lawns
and where our father left us for a while, playing boules in
                                                    the sun.

When he came back he held a clear plastic bag in his hand
with her watch, a locket and a pair of red earrings inside.
They were round, and joined by their clips —
marbles of blood wishboned together.

Skirrid

I. Facing West

She is a she, but I do not know why.
This hare-lipped hill, this broken spine of soil

that stretches across my window
steep-sided, a sinking ship upturned.

Where I stood at Easter,
the Black Mountains shifting their weight in the west,

breathing their storm towards me,
turning a slow cloud down their shoulders

that came to me with hail-shot, straight in my face.
Ant eggs blown in my hair.

II. Facing East

A kestrel tilts on the breeze,
over swollen fields, deciding in the sun,

a dark scales paused in the sky,
hanging in the balance,

until finally it folds and dives, a falling grain,
and is no longer there.

Only the view is left, and in the distance,
the Severn, a long haze

which flexes once a year,
rolling one huge wave down the estuary.

Now though, it is quiet, deciding,
its muscle still growing far out at sea.

Gallery

I. Degas

Head bowed, a woman plays the cello of her hair.
Another bends to complete herself,
moulding her foot with a towel.

Ballerinas fan a haze across their faces,
rest their heads, use their legs as ledges.
One, on her own, plaits her shin with lace.

And through this frame, the artist himself,
smoothing his wrinkles with the brush
of his own short-sightedness.

II. Bonnard

The first room is mostly windows,
reds and yellows swimming round
her naked frame.

Through here, her long body made water,
Ophelia preserved in the bath.

And then this. Self portrait No. 95 (1945)
A Buddha; eyes burnt out
with looking.

III. Hopper

His women wait,
often in sunlight, their white dresses blown,
opaque across the pink of their skin.

Mostly alone, but sometimes with men;
a late night diner, or under a porch,
her shorts pressed to a triangle: his wandering eyes.

But it is not always the city.
Remember the lighthouse, snug in the dunes,
and the yacht, its white sails blown solid across the
                                                    blue sky.

IV. Klimt's Kiss

Or is this Porphyria with her lover?
Him kissing the blood in her cheeks
before it sinks beneath the skin.

Cradling her head at the angle
of a broken neck,
a loose and heavy weight.

His to kiss and keep,
in the gold cloak of his act.
Her kneeling to him in prayer.

World Maps

They call these raised rashes their world maps.
Goose-bump patterns, black on brown,
a disease of the skin, the legacy
of drinking Kava right through the night,
until even the geckoes have swallowed the last of
                                            their voices.

Each man's map is his own, as distinctive as his walk,
or the way he makes love to his wife.
A continent swirls across the shoulders of one,
an archipelago spattered on the arm of another.
A whole country, etched across a chest,
hair for forests, a nipple marking the capital.

Some nights their wives will spill warm coconut oil
into cupped hands,
and flat-palm their husbands' dry bodies.
Or they will walk across their aching backs,
by the light of a hurricane lamp,
the world at their feet, singing to the children.

The Umbilical Tree

I explain.

I have come to find my umbilical tree,
the tree that holds my root in its roots.

She pinches my cheek,
shifts her crossed legs on the floor of someone else's
house,
all these years and still someone else's house.

The sun halves itself in the sea.

I explain.

You are Lor who looked after me,
you buried it here,
after I was born.

You told my parents I would never
forget my roots.
I have not forgotten.

She explains.

She is in someone else's house,
all these years and still someone else's house,
and the tree is gone, plucked by a hurricane years ago.

She says she saw it go, taken like a match in the wind,
that nothing was left,
just a perfect belly button of dark brown soil.

The Fijian Lay Preacher

I

There is a vein in his bicep,
which swells when he works
like a worm beneath the skin.

When he preaches it rises again,
over the tendons in his neck,
emerging from the tightness of his collar.

II

We had worried all night for him,
tight in the corrugate hut,
the rain's fists for a roof.

We were at the birth of thunder,
felt its crack, deep in the ribs,
and its heavy roll in the valley.

We had prepared the fire,
but now the wood was wet charcoal,
and we were losing our faith.

Eventually, the relief of his return;
appearing at the storm's mouth,
holding a bull's head in a bag,

wide from his hip, as easily as a child's hand.

III

He once showed me the marriage pools,
where your choice was made in the throw
of a stone.

Hit the water, you take her.
Hit the rock, you walk alone.

He laughed at the thought
of nervous men, standing on the edge,
sweating into the pebble they held in their hand.

We looked a few moments more,
then walked on,
kicking the stones at our feet.

Mrs Frazer

Once a day, Mrs Frazer, eighty years old,
goes snorkelling on the reef,
which lies like a secret beneath
the dark waters across the road.

She enters in her dress, finding no need for any unpeeling,
or showing of flesh;
she prefers to let the cloth billow about her,
until she floats, face down, in an impression of death.

Sometimes, to swim through a wave,
she will spin on to her side,
but mostly, she just lies still,
resting on the swollen stomach of the tide.

Levi

Levi the cow-herd returns,
down the coastal road,
lop-sided with palm trees
that peck in the wind.
His withered arm hangs high,
a puppet, one string too tight,
and there is a rhythmic beat
beneath his diabetic eye,
from which he looks out across the water
to where a trawler stitches sea to sky.

Levi the cow-herd returns,
to his wife at the door
fresh from Simoni's embrace,
(a man they hire to drive).
His coconut oil has smeared her dress,
beneath which his loving hand
has bruised the skin,
spreading petals of purple over the black.
Levi knows this, and smiles
on his way to the waterfall.

The Medina at Sousse

We had got ourselves lost
in the high stone walls of the medina.

Not in the tourist bit mind,
where women sell authentic sets of chess,

while their child unwraps another
to take the sold one's place.

No, in the quiet areas, further up the hill,
where furballs of kittens crouch

and opened doors reveal men, dicing in groups,
or a naked woman, talcing her toes.

Another, as old as a grandmother
stares from a blue-iron balcony,

her towelling robe giving up its embrace,
to show the long drag of her breasts

and the double fold of her belly;
a frown over one dark eyebrow.

Your hand tightens to a fist in mine,
but I am enjoying this:

I think I am getting the authentic goods —
this part of town where robes shrink to the floor

with a shrug and a step, as women unwrap themselves,
to take the sold one's place.

Sea Reading

for H.M.

Thick skinned in wetsuits, sitting on surf boards,
we are learning to read again,
tracing, in the distance, the phrases of the waves.

Under the sun we watch each swell,
familiarise ourselves with their false promises,
the words that fail to make the page.

We wait, between the speech marks of distant gulls,
between the blank paper of the beach
and the last line of the horizon.

We wait for the sentence of water,
kamikazing itself towards the shore, that will allow us
our fluency,
our moment of balance on the tightrope of the wave,

before it cuts us short, rubs us out
in a diaspora of white water,
leaving us to struggle back through our new language,

back to where, resting in a caesura,
showing only their heads, an ellipsis of seals
tells us it will continue,

but that for now the water is preparing its speech,
drawing upon its vocabulary of waves,
which are still just ideas, growing in the mind of the sea.

River Swimming

Slip into the black dress of the river.

Let go of the bank and slide beneath.
Risk an open eye, feel the ice hit your iris.

Stretch your feet down to touch
the nothingness of its depth.

Feel the fish kiss the hairs on your leg.

Then push through
to the promise of liquid sun.

Taking the air with a massive mouth,
and the wide pull of your lungs.

Lie on these rocks,
soak your shadow onto their dry skin.

Cook from beneath; heat from within.

Night Bus

The girl with glitter in her hair
falls to sleep for a second against a stranger's shoulder,
leaves her mark, star-dust on his collar.

Two women with a mission get on.
They sit next to the lost, the forgotten,
slip their pamphlets into half-curled hands.

She's falling again, her eyes flicking like a faulty screen,
dipping to darkness, sparking to light,
nodding her head in time to her own unconsciousness.

"Look to Jesus and he will save you,
he will show you the path to righteousness, the path to right.
Only he will show you the way."

Finally her head drops, the inky hammer to the paper,
the judge's gavel, falling as slow as only the guilty sees it fall;
but stranger, the young man in Wrangler, doesn't move.

Him and the driver, who counts them in, animals to the ark,
then shuts his doors, which hiss as they close,
a flat glass palm-off to the unsaved outside.

But then he moves his arm, a slow over-arm bowl,
over her resting head, then down across her shoulders,
a denim scarf of late night love, fingers stroking.

They're out of pamphlets, so the two women leave,
but others come to take their places,
sit and watch the scene behind their reflections,
                                    the days credits roll.

Except for Wrangler man, whose own head has dipped now
so he can smell the scent of her hair and kiss her there,
just lightly on the top of her head.

And isn't that what we want anyway?
For love to come to us in our sleep,
to come to us here and now, when we least expect it,
when we need it.

She sinks deeper into her sleep, and deeper into him,
while his eyes watch the closed lids of hers,
and he tries not to disturb her with his breathing.

For love to get on and sit next to us,
to bring a halt to this night bus, and its endless
                                        midnight ellipsis
of stops and stops and stops....

Space Invaders

A confidence of swans,
coming at us with prehistoric necks, the question mark
of head and beak, that bulge beneath the eyes.

Their dodo waddle, so alien
to their usual smooth cut and groove of water,
their aquatic soft-shoe shuffle, their lakeside glide.

Pausing just short, they nonchalantly lift their angel wings,
and peer beneath, reaching for holsters,
before coming on again, somehow taller,

chests low-slung and puffed
above a John Wayne swagger,
a menace hinting in their dark eyes.

You tense in my hand and I try not to tense beside you —
but we are denied the satisfaction of their attack,
and they never touch, make no noise even.

Never threatened with those wings that can snap a
                                        man's back.
Instead, they teach us a lesson in their own silent way,
stretch their necks and pick at the air around us,

confront us with beauty and the promise of pain.
Make no fuss, just pluck at our edges —
then leave us.

Tourette's at the Movies

The white mask of screen light,
sliding over your face
shines up a child's expression:
age slipped off the skin like water,
a single mercury tear mark
blistering the curve of your cheek.
The shutter speed of your lids, slowed to a stare,
renewed once a minute with a blink.

Then the connection; a magnesium strip
dropped across the poles of head and heart.
A shock, thrilled through tensing limbs.
Chin to chest, hand to mouth, elbows dug in the ribs,
spasms of emotion rising to the surface,
pulsing like blood under the skin.

A red fist gathers loose nerves,
waits for the heroine's scream, then tugs,
pulling you tight from within.

A True Story

You have the truth tattooed on your back.
At least, that's what you told me it meant,
a single Japanese symbol
in blue-green ink, high on your shoulder blade,
a spider pretending to be dead.

Sometimes it looks like a mistake,
part hidden by the strap of your dress.
Does that make it a half-truth?
A white lie on your shoulder
ready to whisper into your ear.

Once, when we had argued,
and you had played dumb all day,
you turned your back to me in bed;
forcing me to face the truth,
in a language I will never understand.

The Wedding

We watched them marry,
punctuating the service
with our own long looks
and your finger, twitching in my belt loop.

In the garden, beneath the
surprised arches, you winked
over the rim of a gin,
I kissed my glass in reply.

That night we shared
a row in the street,
shouting promises, exchanging vows.
Windows lit up as witnesses.

A bat blessed us overhead.

History

"...our souls are love, and a continual farewell"
Ephemera, W.B. Yeats

I. Still Point

As you looked out
where the ocean met the evening sky,
then further still,
as if you hoped to slip through
the long seam of the horizon,
I looked at you.

And you will never know
how the light made minerals in your eyes,
which I longed to mine with my own.

II. Morning Glory

After a long night of silence
and backs turned in bed,
you offer up
the forgiveness of your mouth.

In return I give you my medal,
which you wear,
silver and heavy,
slung round the base of your neck.

III. Nobody Home

Two weeks since we agreed to part,
give in to distance, listen to the head
and not the heart,
and here I am again, on the dawn walk home,
through streets of sleet and styrofoam.

Through the door and I check the phone —
you called again at twelve twenty-three.
I was out, trying to lose myself,
trying to shake the you from me.

Eclipse

We watched it apart, and perhaps that was my mistake,
letting the half-darkness fall over you in the city,

while I traced its spreading hand across the fields,
following the rooks, flying in threes to roost.

But as the sun became quarter, then half moon,
it unlocked in me, and I saw us connected again,

by the day's slowing to monochrome, by the mid-day
                                    midnight breeze
and by the moon's shadow passing over and between us.

It was, however, just a trick of the light,
as I learnt, on returning and calling you that night;

listening to your voice down the line,
cooled by his presence, eclipsed and clipped.

And then, on going to sleep, the dream —
his shadow falling across your up-looking face —

his shadow, falling across your memory of me.

Stopped in the Street

It was your mouth which unlocked me
not the dark half-moons of dirt beneath your nails

or the street's cologne, which you wore,
rich and sweet with slept-in grime —

I've built a city side against such things,
used now, to keeping pain in the corner of my eye.

But your mouth, down and out in your face,
full with the pebble of absence, chewing on air,

stuck, the jaw repeating on a sound, scratched
somewhere in your head; I had to stop for that,

feeling once more the catch of consonants in the throat,
and the stubborn implosives, packed with potential behind
                                              clenched teeth.

And that is why, in the silence that you spoke,
I dropped those coins into your up-reached palm,

if for nothing else, to hear their chink,
their completed sound carried home, the simple sentence
                                              of money

which you busked from me without knowing,
singing as you did my secret signature tune so well.

May Ball

The bow tie is unfamiliar,
awkward as a fish beneath the chin.
My fingers slip on the knot, poke
the Adam's apple back into my throat.

Suddenly, in the mirror, I see
my grandfather's wedding photo.
Thin with quinsy, his hair like
combed hay, stacked in one corner to dry.

Serious as a mourner, tucked into tails
beside his new wife, he is giving nothing away;
though sixty years later he would tell me
how he felt on that day.

How his proud heart almost broke
his ribs, because the best girl in town
was hooked on the crook of his arm,
her soft fingers under his hard hand.

But here, in creeping sepia,
he is giving nothing away,
stare starched as his shirt,
mouth, tight and neat as his tie.

*

The braces fastened, shoes buffed
the waistcoat with no back tied,
I come through the kitchen,
its debris of washing marooned in the sink.

You walk in from the overgrown garden.
The evening shining behind you,
highlighting your pinned-up hair,
and your white dress, low to the ground.

Your unburdened neck amazes me.
A long vase of smooth skin,
braided beneath with tendons,
that twine when you turn, ribbons on a maypole.

I approach you, careful in this hired suit.

*

The queue of heads outside the college shuffle and tilt,
strain to see the noise at the end of the street.

A crowd bunches there, moving as one,
fly-postered placards high.

One mouth blossoms over a policeman's shoulder:
CLASS WAR, FUCK THE RICH.

A burn in my chest spreads to my cheek
as I wait there, in line and out of place.

Under the arch I hand over the tickets;
someone gives me champagne in return.

*

They are making peace in the cloisters,
a string quartet to accompany the flurries
of doves, from eave to wooden eave.

In the "*Virgin* snow quad", fake flakes
fall on girls who weave with trays,
shots of vodka shaking at their shoulders.

On stage the hypnotist clicks his fingers
in time to the blinks of his "helper":
Think of your favourite song....

*

We take the winding stone steps,
up towards the echo of our own feet.

The top room is a bathroom;
you open the window, arms high,

and your back dimples, flexes
in the white strip light.

Pausing above it all,
we smoke our breaths into the night,

until you begin to slide, telling me
it's all right, the floor is clean,

raising your long dress in your hands,
'til it rests, in folds, over your knees.

And I begin to lose myself; in the laser show,
spinning images over the old stone wall;

in the vodka, tapping at my temples,
beating in my veins;

in the doves, safe in their eaves,
in the *Virgin* girls,

in you and your dress,
and the dirt on your knees,

in the crowd in the street
that moves as one,

in the mouth that grows slow
over the shoulder,

in my grandfather, in tails
who gave nothing away,

and in me, who is giving it all.

Leavings

The wind's year-long whisper
has worn the leaves thin.
They turn from their branches,
lend the river a skin.

An easy-flexing eczema,
a dead, patched complexion.
Their beauty is in the falling,
their has-been, their never again.

Acknowledgements

Acknowledgements are due to the following magazines and anthologies in which some of the poems in this collection first appeared: *Poetry Wales, Poetry Ireland, This is..., The Reader, Are You Talking To Me?* (Pont Books, 1994), *Take 20* (CCPA, 1998) and *First Pressings* (Faber, 1998).

I am grateful to The Society of Authors for an Eric Gregory Award, and to *Vogue* for the 1999 Vogue Young Writer's Award.

Thanks are also due to the following for their advice, support, words and wine: Natalie Acton, Pele Cox, Peter Florence, Jake Kemp, Robert Minhinnick, Andrew Motion, Martin Ouvry, Neil Rollinson, Anna Saltmarsh, Amy Wack, Roisin Wesley, Nerys Williams and my brothers Dilwyn and Hywel.

A special thanks to Sarah, who wrote many of these without knowing it.